kissing it all

thanks to:

joolz
and dean at ak.

cover design by boff.

kissing it all

AK
PRESS

teve pottinger

Copyright   Steve Pottinger

First Printing   1996

ISBN 1 873176 32 5

Published by AK Press

PO Box 12766
Edinburgh
EH8 9YE

PO Box 40682
San Francisco
CA 94140-0682

British Library Cataloging-in-Publication Data
A CIP catalogue record for this book is
available from the British Library

Library of Congress Cataloging-in-Publication
Data
A catalogue record for this title is available
from the Library of Congress

Printed by Calvert's Press (TU)
0171 739 1474

contents.

13th floor.

and i remember
him opening the front door
saying come in, make yourself at home.
wanting to show it off, like you do
with a new place.
and walking into a big bare lounge,
not a stick of furniture in it,
just a mustard-coloured carpet
and a view out over leeds.
thinking shit, that's depressing.
thank god i don't live here.
but knowing what it means to him.

him putting stuff away in the kitchen,
pulls 2 litres of martini, 12 cans of brew
out of the shopping bags saying
well i cut a bit loose at the weekends.
takes a can of glue from the bottom,
sees my face, says
only a pint a day now,
used to be six or seven.
me thinking jesusfuckingchrist.
and no smack at all, he says,
rolling his sleeves way up
showing home-made tattoos that spell
glasgow.
see? no tracks.

and him asking what'll it be?
brew? glue? martini?
me saying no, really.
him thinking i was trying to be polite

and me thinking it's a quarter to ten
in the fucking morning.
showing me round:
bathroom, bedroom, toilet,
look i've got a cupboard.
me saying yeah, that's great.

and back in the lounge
him handing me a letter.
saying i wrote to the blood people
see if i could give.
told them no more needles
just a little bit of glue,
nothing like i used to do.
and me seeing someone's written to him
personally,
saying sorry. no we can't,
but thanks for the offer,
all the best and good luck.
and i look up
and he's grinning and scratching his head
happy and embarrassed and full of hope,
and after everything he's been through
still so innocent,
which you don't really think of with junkies.
and me knowing the odds are stacked
way, way against him,
that the walls will close in
or the dss will forget to treat him
like a human being,
and wanting to give him a huge great hug
and tell him steve, i am so fucking proud of
you.
so that he might remember
when the time comes.

8

and him unscrewing the martini
levering the lid off the can of glue,
the moment gone.

and me going back down in the lift,
out to the dogshit and the broken glass,
hoping against hope he has a chance.
him gazing out the window over leeds,
watching the lights dance.

simon.

simon's the life and soul of the party.
the life and soul of the fucking party.
at least that's what simon thinks,
and after a gram or two of whizz
and a hatful of drinks
who can tell? he may be right.
but he stinks of tennents extra
and the promise of a fight.
simon thinks he's jack the lad.
his little circle of mates say he means no harm
he's not that bad.

even at school he was big for his age.
i remember an older lad picked on him once,
a mistake. simon flew into a rage
and beat him bloody,
found himself the object of respect and awe
for just about the first time in his life.
he liked that. wanted more.
and some of us were there to egg him on.
simon's effortless arrogant strength
somehow made us invulnerable,
or at least made life more fun.

we've moved on. he's still jumping
through the same old hoops.
sizing up a stranger
moves in, puts his arm around their
shoulders,
you can see them feel the danger
as the minutes that he's with them
stretch forever.

10

his mates snigger in the background.
they think it's fine
because simon brings back wine
or beer or money or maybe sells a little hash
to someone who doesn't really want
the shit he sells
but thought they'd rather part with cash
than face the threat of anything... else.
but then like his mates say
it's all in fun.
simon never actually hits anyone.
well, hardly ever.

you know that there's a simon
in so many pubs, so many towns.
sad king of a pathetic castle
in a tawdry crown
propping up his ego by scaring
who he can
and sidekicks who think they're hard
because they know a hard man.
happy to live in his shadow.

simon and i go back a long way.
we were never mates,
moving in separate directions
to different fates,
but we knew each other,
each other's news.
the last i heard he'd had a son.
i thought it might change him for the better,
i was wrong. he's getting worse.
he's older now, more desperate,
resents other people's fun,
and what i'd prayed to never see:

he's vicious.
brutal, cruel, losing control.
sees a slight in everything
when the speed takes hold.

last time we met there was a scrap.
nothing very glorious - these things
never are.
just a flurry of fists and adrenalin,
insults and home truths,
blood, nothing broken, the odd bruise.
over.
then the police found simon coming back
from the car with a wheel brace.
last thing i heard him shout was
" i'll smash your fucking face. "
he's got a fistful of nothing
which he thinks he can't afford to lose.
the crown's slipping, slipping, slipping,
and even the booze
can't hide that fact from him.

and me i wonder about the kid
about what he sees and learns
watching daddy being the life and soul
of the party.
daddy being the life and soul
of the fucking party.

festive season.

christmas, she said.
christmas was always the worst.
dad's rough hands,
his breath of tobacco and brandy,
first the pain, and then the numbness.
christmas was washing herself clean
and never succeeding,
praying for festivities to end.

the queen's speech, she says,
the national anthem on the tv,

and nowhere to hide.

godsell.

so on the 3rd or the 4th or the 6th
- or whichever day it was -
god created the human body.
naked, that we might be ashamed
and cover it in embarrassment.
nothing plunging, no provocative hemlines.
out of sight and out of mind.
am i right?

and he said i can sleep with whoever i want.
just the one.
of the opposite gender.
as long as we're married
and aren't seen to take too much pleasure
in the act itself
or try anything the neighbours find kinky
or weird.
fuck with the lights on
and our eyes open.
grim, determined.
that's what you're saying?
and buy myself a nice house
and keep my head down.
give caesar everything caesar asks for.
ask no awkward questions
about who caesar cheats or shoots or starves
to put the morning coffee on my table
just concentrate on getting the kids
through college
and worry about those hemlines.
rich men and camels and needles,
that was a metaphor, yeah?

14

the basics sound like a barrel of fun.
now that bit about how your god can set me
free,
run that past me one more time.
say it with a straight face like you mean it.
to help you along
we'll both pretend you believe it.

window.

my friend rings from london. she says he
came back last night, in through the window.
without bothering to open it first. he came in
through the window because she'd changed
the locks and he couldn't use the door now.
and he stood there, eyes glazed if you'll
pardon the pun, stood there in the broken
glass saying how he'd come to see if there
was any post. i suppose he had the knife to
open envelopes, i suppose that's what he
would have said if she'd thought to ask or if
he'd have thought it needed any justification.

now whether he was letting her know she
wasn't safe no matter what she did, or
whether in his illness he was snatching for
some seemingly reasonable explanation for
what he was doing, an explanation that
would convince them both that he wasn't as
strung-out as he seemed, i don't know. but
my friend is scared, and she doesn't want to
be alone, so i pack a few things onto the bike
and set off down the A1 under cotton-wool
clouds and the smell of fresh grass, new
growth after a long winter. and as i ride, i
think of my two friends. my friend who is
terrified for her life now, and my other friend
who carries a knife and walks through
windows....

if anyone had told me a few months back that
this is how he would react when the

16

relationship fell apart, i'd have laughed them out of court. quiet, gentle mick, the vegan with green fingers, raving like something mad and broken? scaring women? get a grip.

but he is. tells her how much he still loves her, how he can't possibly live without her, how she must see that all he wants to do is make her happy... then how he can't bear to lose her, how he'll kill any man who shares her bed with her, that's how much he loves her. he's already scared one guy off with phone calls and the knife. now he's walking through windows, as if that will somehow win her back....

as the bike carries me towards london, i search through my memories to see if there's anything i can find which might help to explain mick's behaviour, thinking to myself that if i could just latch onto something i could hate him like everyone else seems to, but i can't.

she won't come back. and he can't change it. i think that's what hurts him most. if he got her back he'd hate her guts within a week and finish it just like he did last time, not being able to make believe any more that the rows and fights and days they couldn't stand each other never really happened. which is what he's doing now, pleading with her to make his life all better, then pulling a knife when she doesn't fall in line.

17

if he'd just walk away, he could start to pull
his life back together. sleep a little. learn to
eat again. and i wish he would. and i know
he won't, and that he and i will become
enemies because one day i'll meet up with
him and have to tell him what he's doing is
wrong and he's going to see this as betrayal.
and maybe there'll be a fight and maybe i'll
win and maybe i won't and probably nothing
will change.

and i speed down the A1 and arrive in
london, tasting the air pollution, and i think
about mick and about how lonely and
desperate and totally fucked-up you have to
be when you find yourself walking through
windows. i want to find him and reach out to
him, because he is my friend and he's
hurting, and i know that it probably won't be
possible. and the pollution here today is
worse than usual, it must be, because it's
difficult to swallow, and my eyes are stinging
and full of tears. and i slip through the traffic
to find my other friend, who's hurting too,
thinking to myself how most everyone i
know is messed up one way or another; how
much of our time we spend helping each
other through another crisis, another broken
heart. picking up the pieces and hoping to
make something that works. full of good
intentions, too clumsy to make them true.

and how sometimes it's never enough.

but it's all we've got.

18

a packet of dreams
and a bottle of strongbow.

i was in a band once, for about six months.
every saturday afternoon we'd head off to a
mate's dad's friend's garage near the waste
ground where the factories had been, set up
the drum kit and the amps and get wrecked
on cheap dry cider and grass bought from the
local rastas. in all that time we never played a
gig. i'm not sure we even had a name. we
just spent saturday afternoons thrashing out
something loud and tuneless for a few hours,
having fun.

we weren't bothered about being cool. which
was just as well: this was walsall, it was
1980, people still wore flared jeans with deep
purple patches, and the burning fashion
question was whether you should or
shouldn't have tassles on the back of your
leather jacket. we'd swig at the cider and
argue the toss about which black sabbath
album had made the most lasting contribution
to the world of rock music... like we were
spoilt for choice... and now and then we'd
destroy a much-loved tune. sabbath
usually....

at our best, we were hopeless. i couldn't play
bass to save my life, no-one could sing, and
although the drummer had been in other
bands and could keep time, poor sod, the

19

guitarists' only aim in life was to play bigger
louder guitar chords than anyone in the
history of big loud guitar chords, ever. so
mostly we were worse than hopeless, and by
the end of an afternoon of cider and spliffs,
hopelessness wouldn't have touched us with
a bargepole.

we dreamt of stardom, all the same. believed
that somehow in our wasted, fogged saturday
afternoons we'd stumble across **that tune**,
the one that would catapult us up and away
from a town where the factories had closed,
and into something... i don't know... full of
drugs and fast women, i suppose. it was just
a matter of being discovered... and then we'd
escape from walsall with music and guitars,
like we imagined our heroes had done before
us. god, we knew nothing.

for a while though, ignorance was bliss, and
we forgave each other anything. it didn't
matter that i couldn't play, or that pez always
hogged the spliff, or that pete never put any
cash in but took his share and more, or that
stu was a loudmouth and a bore when he got
pissed; we were all part of the great escape
together, and people would be so jealous of
us when we left our smalltown behind,
because we were going to do it....

and then we grew up and learnt about the
world a bit and realised it was never going to
happen, and the whole thing disintegrated in
backbiting and petty hate. the drummer

discovered jesus, joined a cheesy rock-gospel band and cut us dead. the last time i saw him was as i waited for a bus in the town centre and he said "hallo sinner" as he passed. pez bought the axe hero myth, you know, lots of drugs and the harder the better, got laid on the strength of it, and ended up working fitting tyres. stu? i don't know what happened to stu. he disappeared into exams and a career and the normality we'd sworn to avoid back in the days when we didn't know shit. i was lucky. and bloody-minded. and here i am.

and every now and then i think of those saturday afternoons when strongbow tasted of freedom, and sabbath ruled, and i remember how we hadn't learned to be cool, and we hadn't learned to pretend we didn't care, and we chased the beauty of our dreams...

and maybe we snatched at something never meant for such as us, who knows? but we weren't cool.

at least we were never cool.

dreamtime.

and today
the talk on the bus
is of who got shot in the head last night
and why. what he did to deserve it.
" you know him. he was a mate of..."

when i was a small boy i dreamed
of being a fireman astronaut engine driver.
heroic, glamorous, exciting,
as the dreams of small boys are.

older,
i dreamed of justice.
i dreamed of justice.
damages mended, hurts healed, wrongs
righted.
to each of us according to our needs.
that way, i thought, all of us can dream....
justice was one small word.
it didn't seem much to ask.

now i sit on the bus,
listen to this conversation
without shock, without anger,
never even asking myself
if the dead man dreamed of driving engines
or in another, better world,
what his killer might have been.

and i wonder if this has become
the best of our futures,
this casual chatter of guns, bullets, death.

i wonder at how far we've come
that i don't even catch my breath
or pause for a moment.

while dreams of justice
echo hollow and empty in my head.

euro96.

somewhere someone's playing football.
the dss office queue is long.
the fat girl in front of me screams
at her small child
i think because she can.
someone leaves.
we all take one step forward.

there is, i understand,
much talk of a feelgood factor.

dog.

seems that more and more i watch the strong
get stronger and the weak turn on themselves;
there are days when i don't see it ever getting
any better. i try and ignore it and i can't, it's
not the way i am. instead it eats at me, at my
peace of mind, leaves me depressed and
furious, hopeless and full of rage.
everywhere i look i see injustice....

the other monday morning i spent a lifetime
on the phone listening to the voice on the
other end telling me rules are rules are rules
are rules. i bit my tongue so i wouldn't call it
a fucking idiot and wheedled and cajoled and
buttered it up and made it feel important, and
all the while i knew in my heart it was so
much wasted breath.

my friends jim and sally, they're retarded,
they're not the full quid. they moved into a
maisonette on one of the estates together, and
then they got burgled and she lost the kid she
was carrying. so jim bought the dog.
something to make her feel safe. something
for her to love. you don't need to be able to
read to know what to do at times like this.

they thought it was cruel to keep it in the
house all day, so they let it run free. they
stopped putting collars on it, because it didn't
like collars. with the benefit of hindsight it
was only a matter of time till the dog warden

picked it up. and when jim looked out of the window and saw him put the dog in the back of the van, he ran out to explain

and the warden told him to stick it, and drove away.

which is why i was on the phone, trying to get it back. listening to a voice which would hear of no excuses, no mitigating circumstances. jim had 5 days to pay a £60 fine, and if he only gets £90 a fortnight that's not the voice's problem, is it?

jim wanted me to make everything right again, and i couldn't. now he gets angry, shouts at me, tells me it's kidnap and it's murder... and he's right. he's bright enough to understand that what's happening is wrong, whatever the rules say. sally just sees that the dog she loves, and which loved her, has been taken away, and she wants it back, which isn't much to ask, so why isn't it happening?

and i put the phone down and i hadn't got an answer for them, nothing that makes sense, nothing that's decent or honest or good. and it won't make the headlines, and the voice probably thinks of itself as being a good man, doing his best, caring for his family, salt of the earth and all that. and all i know is that the strong have stopped protecting the weak, if they ever did, and that somewhere a girl cries herself to sleep every night, and that

jim drinks himself stupid, and nurses a
grievance, and tries to forget that he could do
nothing, and i go home on the bus to news of
war and no longer believe we deserve any
better.

lament.

my friend is a junkie.
he's going to give it up. he says so.
when he leaves for rome,
milan, paris, san francisco.
wherever it is takes his fancy this week.
this is my friend,
who barely leaves the house anymore.

my friend is a junkie.
he does it to numb his feelings.
used to claim he smoked but didn't shoot,
now he just denies he's dealing.

my friend is a junkie.
he has the whiny junkie mentality
about how no-one really loves him,
no-one understands.
then slips £10 out of your purse
when you're not looking.

my friend is a junkie.
one day he tells me
he hasn't touched the stuff
for, oh, must be weeks.
and i want to believe him.
i want to believe him.
then i find the works hidden in the bathroom.

my friend is a junkie.
says he has it under control.
then goes out and robs his own house.
but how else do you find £40 a day?

28

my friend is a junkie.
i've tried everything:
persuasion, anger, argument,
tears rolling down my face.
none of it does any good.
he loves the drug more than he loves me.
it always gives him what he thinks he wants.

my friend is a junkie.
he tells me william burroughs is a junkie too.
that's all right then.
it must be me who's not being cool.

my friend is a junkie.
and it scares me.
some days i want to lose myself too,
escape, give up. the desire for addiction
tastes metal on my tongue
and i think... well... maybe....

my friend is a junkie.
i don't let him in my flat.
i know most what he tells me is lies.
i know that when i walk away
he'll use that as another excuse
to be a junkie.

our friendship distant,
fading into memory.

harvest.

summer was slipping away, and as the
evenings drew in, my friend and i drifted
south out of amsterdam, following the sun.
we'd heard of work harvesting the grapes in
france, and we hitched our way down there,
eking out the last of our money, basking in
the warmth of a mediterranean august, not
ready yet to go home.

looking back now, i find it hard to believe we
did it, you know, just headed off without a
care in the world. the hardest thing about
travelling has always been shutting the front
door behind you; then you've cut yourself
free, for better or worse, and nothing that
happens after that seems quite as bizarre or
threatening as it does when you relate it to the
ones who stayed at home. still, knowing
what i know now, i wouldn't have the same
peace of mind if i did it again. then i was
arrogant and young: we were lucky, too
stupid to be scared. or maybe it was
innocence that saw us through. who knows?

anyway, we meandered south and pitched up
in a market town full of streetside cafes and
the smell of croissants. somewhere more
typically french you couldn't imagine. it was
busy enough in a provincial kind of way, but
the heavy trucks and tourist coaches sped
past along the autoroute on the other side of
the river, leaving it lazy and timeless.only

30

transient workers like us ever visited, hunting
down a living.

and we weren't alone. in a square off the
main street we found others, english mainly,
surprisingly enough. there was a soldier gone
awol, a couple of his mates, some others i
don't remember, and there was jamie and
tara.

jamie was on the run, but then a lot of people
were. it's just that he'd been up for gbh - "oh
i did it " he said - and i couldn't quite imagine
that, however hard i tried. it just didn't add
up. jamie was a live wire, sure, but he was
so slightly built, so gentle by nature.... he
was fun to be around, and we warmed to him
as everyone else did. i instinctively trusted
him.

so did tara, obviously. small and blonde,
she'd met jamie when she went out to tenerife
for two weeks with some friends. jamie had
been selling timeshare then, and living well
on it. there'd been a fortnight of drink, drugs
and parties, and when the plane left for
home, tara wasn't on it. "nothing to go back
to, was there?" she said. "man, who wants
to be a clerk all their life?" and i knew what
she meant. jamie was exciting, he made
things happen. even we felt that.

so we hung round with them, and they
showed us the ropes. we spent the days
busking, begging, hanging round the little

square with its fountain, and in the evening
we got drunk. someone found out that
apparently, by napoleonic law, you couldn't
get done for nicking food, except booze and
fags, and so immediately we started eating a
lot better. jamie and tara went to a
supermarket one day and the manager met
them outside, said he knew what they were
up to, and he'd rather give 'em stuff than
have them nick it, then handed over carrier
bags of bread, cheese and fruit. it was typical
of the way they landed on their feet, just
typical, and everyone laughed when they got
back and wondered out loud just what tara
had had to do to make the supermarket
manager so generous, and she blushed and
told us all to fuck off, and we shared
everything out between us.

but we were always short of money. i stood
outside the church one sunday evening, head
bowed, hands held out as the people left after
mass. the soldier had told me it was a sure
bet, but i didn't make much, and it was so
embarrassing i went straight back to busking
next day, juggling for hours on end and
making just about enough for some bread and
cheese and wine. the soldier, meanwhile,
was walking out of shops with bottles of
spirits, despite the risk, and one afternoon he
and his mates got slowly wasted on stolen
whisky and they cut a cyst out of his back
with a swiss army knife to pass the time.

ten days, maybe two weeks passed like this.

32

every evening we'd pool our money and sit
round the fountain drinking cheap red wine
till we had no more and laugh about how
much fun we were having and didn't this beat
having a job, and how we'd be back next
year eating in the posh restaurant in the
square and where would we go in the
meantime, and then we'd crawl into our
sleeping bags and pass out. i remember jamie
and tara said they'd go back to tenerife, and
we said we fancied north africa. it all seemed
possible then, you know, i think we all
thought it was really possible.

it was drawing to an end though, we knew it,
and we wrung every enjoyment we could
from our last few days of freedom. i guess
that mainly meant we got drunker than ever.
tara had taken up tapping people directly for
cash; i mean she was so small and cute no-
one could resist her, and when funds or
booze were short she would wander the main
street and the square smiling sweetly, then
returning with a bottle or two of the cheap red
wine we'd grown to love.

so when she disappeared again, we thought
nothing of it. and when she came back, i
didn't notice any difference, not at first. but
jamie did. as if he were telepathic. "who?" he
asked, and when she didn't answer,
"where?" i looked at her now. she was
trembling, shaking, deep in shock. "toilets"
she choked. a tear rolled down her cheek,
and she curled up on herself, sobbing.

i couldn't quite piece this together, but jamie
was up and off, running across the square,
screaming "bastard! you fucking bastard!"
he was a different person now, and i think it
scared him. it made the hair stand up on the
back of my neck, and my stomach turn. and
the guy coming out of the toilets, well when
he saw jamie racing for him, he ran back
inside and locked himself in.

so there was this standoff. jamie banging at
the door, screaming, trying to rip it off its
hinges, and the guy with no intention of
letting him anywhere near him, calling to his
mates for help. they came running and we
blocked their way. "it's not your fight" we
told them, "not your fight." and squared up
uneasily. it could have gone on all night:
jamie kicking at the door, tara sobbing, most
of us not really too sure what was going on,
but sticking with our mates come hell or high
water. and it did. it did.

a french lad with us had a cs gas canister, for
personal protection, like they do. and he gave
it to jamie, and jamie rolled it under the door.
i was 20 feet away, and my eyes ran, my
throat stung. for the guy inside it must have
been impossible, but he stayed where he
was, knowing full well what was waiting for
him. and jamie stayed too, though he must
have been barely able to breathe inside the
confines of the toilet block where the fumes
were most intense.

and when the guy came out, jamie took a
bottle to him, one of the bottles of cheap red
that tara had spent her evenings tapping for.
he carved the guy's face to ribbons. raving at
him, kicking him, cutting him again and
again and again with the sharp broken glass.
he'd have killed him, i think, if the foul air
hadn't driven him out. and given the guy a
chance to stagger away pouring more blood
than i'd ever seen. or wish to see again.

the police came, of course. the restaurant
owner called them, a riot on his doorstep not
being too good for trade, i guess. but it was
all over, and they contented themselves with
just moving everyone on, making them
gather their few possessions and leave. it was
just another fight between the transients and a
local arab, and they didn't much care for
either. the rape didn't make it that different.
and although i do remember a policewoman
talking to tara, asking her if she wanted to
press charges, they seemed quite relieved
when she didn't. what with the need for a
translator and all that. they just gave us a few
extra minutes and asked us to move on too.

and we left, the four of us. walked through
the night. jamie saying to me over and over,
"i did right didn't i? i did right? i had to do it.
for tara. i had to. i'd do it again, the bastard.
fuck, man, tell me i did right." because it had
happened to tara before, before she'd ever
met him, which was why she didn't want to
talk to the police, knowing about the

examination, the probing, the look in their eyes that asked just why a pretty young girl would be approaching strange men anyway.... she wasn't having any of it, and she wrapped jamie's fierce and furious love round her for warmth and protection and wanted that to be enough.

and we walked for hours, almost till daybreak, out of the town to the river. and we found a small park and a hut and tried to sleep, tried to comfort tara, tried to calm jamie. wanted to rewind time, to heal the hurt, to make it all clean and perfect and full of laughter like it had been. and we finished the wine to drown the anger and woke up next morning, empty, bitter, and old, and went looking for work.

nomad.

i am sleeping in the van on a remote headland
in orkney. the headland is at the end of a
farm-track which winds its way here from
where the single-track road ends. the single-
track road has, in turn, led on from another
single-track road, and at the other end of that
single-track road is the middle of nowhere.

i sit in the van, which rocks gently from the
constant buffeting of the wind sweeping in
from the great northern seas. i gaze out at the
impossible beauty of a midsummer sunset, at
a panorama of sea, other islands, islets, the
immensity of an ever-changing sky. all i can
hear is the call of seabirds, the breaking of
waves on the rocks below. from here, the
city i live in seems some diseased imagining,
born of some other nightmare world.

half a mile away there is a house. one day i
stop to talk to the woman who lives there
with her dogs. she is elderly and south
african. but how did you get here? i ask,
gesturing at the farm-track, the twisting
single-track roads, the half a planet that
stretches back beyond them to her homeland.

oh, she says, as if it explains everything,

i came via barnsley.

kidding myself, again.

i've been doing it for months now.
living as if this was a rehearsal
for something greater,
as if i can live this life without beauty
and it doesn't matter.
telling myself that if i ignore my feelings
as long as i can
there'll be something good on tv
and i can lose myself in that again.
it's bullshit.
and i know it.
but still catch myself hoping
that if i numb myself for long enough
i won't be aware of that
or anything.
it will all slip by in a dream.
there will be no pain....

i wonder who i think i'm kidding,
blaming her for leaving me,
telling myself everyone hates me,
then being so surly that i make that true.
oh, there are days when it all comes clear
and i know that's what i do
and i promise myself i'll change
right now, tomorrow, next week...
my good intentions slip away
it's easier to stay the same.

rather that than try
and make a fool of myself.

someone ought to punch me square between
the eyes
scream at me,
provoke a reaction,
something, anything to free this log jam.
i know i've said i'll put down anyone
who tries,
but i still wish they would.
when did i learn that if someone hits you
then they love you?
how? and why?

oh, none of it's important.
i've a roof over my head, haven't i?
beer in the fridge,
channels to flick through.
what's the word? surf?
slumped in my chair telling my friends
one day i'll get it all together

kidding myself.

seen, not heard.

imagine a child
seeing everything new and magical
unfolding endlessly
before its open, eager eyes.

imagine the slaps, the beatings,
the bruises, the tears,
the repetition of how bad,
how stupid, how ugly, how naughty
little johnny, little jane is,
how mommy and daddy are
terribly disappointed,
sigh, after all they've done....

watch wariness creep in,
a hard sheen,
or a need to please,
a cold edge,
like ice forming.
whatever it takes for survival.
dreams are only dreams.

imagine a child as a television:

now tell me
you'd buy one
then put a fist through the screen.

urban spaceman.

danny is roaring up the town again,
flying on sherry and glue.
size of an ox, headful of scrambled eggs.
bouncing off lampposts,
scaring the pensioners,
huge and free and dirty and laughing to
himself.

and depending on what he's been mixing the
booze with -
i don't know, perhaps the light changes,
something shifts within his skull -
say hello to danny the urban nightmare.
this shithouse, staring at nothing,
stands in the middle of the street,
stops the traffic,
screams at everyone,
and takes on double-decker buses.

and i think he's screaming
for the home he left when just fourteen,
for sucking off strangers
in anonymous cars,
for the lives he sees on tv that'll never be his,
for pills and booze, pills and booze.
i think he's screaming
for the hopeless shuffle:
hostel, day centre, cell.
screaming because the pain is too huge to be
silent.

and it takes six policemen

to get him into the back of the van
because danny's a big strong lad
who isn't giving a flying fuck about
anything.

and when he's slept it off,
had his first square meal for a couple of days,
and a handful of roll-ups,
they ask him what he thinks he's playing at
without really expecting an answer.
i mean when he's straight
he hasn't the first idea himself,
so how's he going to explain it to them?

we've been sending men to the moon
since before he could talk,
and no-one's sent danny anywhere.
except in and out of armley,
which wasn't much of a giant step for
anybody.
so now he leaves for planet dan
whenever he can.
easy enough to get there -
just the price of a bottle and whatever
anyone's holding.
most things blur the fury,
nothing much helps him dream.

and i know no-one's to blame.
that it's the way the cards fall,
nothing more,
that progress dances to a different tune
you have to see the bigger picture,
and i'd like to go on record
as expressing my appreciation for

the space shuttle the channel shuttle
the worldwide burger

but still i know
that a week after i begin this poem
danny will throw himself under a bus,
that leeds is sometimes like space
no-one hears you scream,
and that sherry and glue
were as near as he got to flying.

life's a pub.

cheryl walks in wearing bruises,
says she fell into a door.
no-one takes much notice.
they've heard that line so many times before.
she brings rumours of an overdose,
but it's no-one from round here
just another place where we don't go,
with water in the beer.
she heads for don and tony
who are on the nod
smacked out smacked out smacked out - god!
someone turns and tells you
they're the best days of our lives.
you laugh and say that's bullshit,
but a small voice says they could be right.

there's a stranger in the taproom
being overly polite.
the couple standing next to him
are spoiling for a fight:
she's looking daggers
and he's looking pissed
hate is tattooed in her eyes
just like it's tattooed on his fist.
the boys are in the backroom talking war,
every friday night about 9 o'clock they say
they won't take this shit no more,
then at 20 past 11 the door shuts in their faces
and rebellious intent
becomes a piss in public places.
a kebab, a curry, home,
shagging other men's wives

desperately believing
they're the best days of their lives.

jane is sitting on the bar stool, looking cool,
dressed to thrill,
dreams of love that never happens,
then goes home and takes her pills,
to help her sleep and keep her calm
so the next night she'll be there again,
sitting at the bar.
tasha has a kid at home,
she keeps it quiet with booze,
it wears hand-me-down clothes
and oxfam shoes.
then she goes out and sells herself
to pay the rent.
well what's a girl to do?
when the giro's spent.
and yvette, the pretty girl, who cuts herself,
well sometimes strangers try it on,
till they see something screaming in her eyes
and they drink up and they're gone,
moving on and looking
for the best days of their lives

and there's a rumble at the back door
and the flash of knives,
could be over a girl or dodgy gear,
but there's nothing much to see.
shouts and scuffles, someone does a runner,
at least it's better than tv.
there's a frisson of excitement,
we can live on this for days,
the jukebox playing fast and loud
in a hash-smoke haze.

some old guy's passed out in the corner
but no-one cares,
we just carry on around him
like he wasn't there.
beer and fags and laughter,
some whizz and down the club.
you're a fool to expect something more.
i tell you, life's a pub.

in the club, the music deafens you,
the spotlight blinds your eyes.
you can't remember what your dreams were,
or when you kissed them all goodbye.
it's 2am. you stagger home.
the helicopter in the sky
is watching us all having

the best days of our lives.

new world.

once in a blue moon,
days like this one dawn,
i remember why i love this town.
frost beneath our feet,
above, a clear pale winter sky.
the sun skids across the rooftops,
cannot burn, but blinds.
ice and fire turn everything
to white and gold, white and gold.

and here on the top deck of the bus,
the old drunk singing hymns
to the glory of tennents,
smoking a rollie and sod the cancer,
buildings slip by like strangers,
people pass like dreams.
the world outside commonplace, yet magical.

and it seems it might be possible
to start again, clean, unsullied,
no longer trailing our disappointments
behind us.

at the end of the street
the moors hang over us, a promise.

art of war.

2000 years ago a chinese warrior, sun tzu,
wrote of the art of war. how you win most
easily by never entering into conflict
yourself, but let your enemy tire himself out
in the field, expose his weaknesses while you
keep yourself hidden, safe and secure. how
you surprise attack when least expected, how
you never let him be confident of
understanding your tactics, how you keep
him guessing, always keep the upper hand.

and you storm into the pub, raving about
sandy, telling anyone who'll listen that this
time you've had it with the bitch, had it with
her moods, her silences, had it with her
slamming the phone down when you ring to
try and make the peace after the last row, had
it with her full stop. you can do better, you
tell us. it's not as if there haven't been
offers.... man, but is she ever fucking up,
losing you.

and you're right, of course. you probably
could do better, and there may even have
been offers. but nothing's going to change.
you'll sit here in the pub with us, drinking
pint after pint till you've taken the head off
your fury, cataloguing the endless injustices
that sandy has done to you, while we nod
non-commitally, waiting, waiting.

and sure enough, about half an hour before

48

closing you lean close to me, elbows on the
table, swaying over your pint, your voice
plaintive and childlike, and tell me that you
love her. and if i could stuff the words back
in your mouth, i would. you try your best,
you tell me, but you're too selfish, too
demanding, you never show your love.
maybe you should buy her something, maybe
you should move in together, maybe that's
what she needs....

and i sip at my pint and hope to conceal my
feelings, wishing you'd shut up, thinking
how tired i am of hearing about you and
sandy, and that you must be the only person
on the planet who doesn't know about her
and jake, and then out of nowhere you ask if
she's sleeping with anyone, and if i knew i'd
tell you, wouldn't i? and i'm still opening my
mouth and wondering why i should have to
be the one to tell you, wondering if i will
anyway, and i realise you aren't waiting for
an answer, thank god, you're mumbling
about a meal out, flowers, whatever.

and i think about sun tzu, and think to myself
that i could never see your relationship with
sandy as having very much to do with love

but viewed as war it makes perfect sense.

true romance.

paul looks after annie the best he can.
o.k. so they do a bit of glue but man
you do what you have to do to get by,
and if it means you get out of it,
means you get high,
then that's the way it is.
i mean, it's not like anyone cares.

take now, outside the station, people stare
at paul like he crawled from underneath a
rock.
he's way past giving a fuck about this.
so the "hungry and homeless" sign
isn't strictly legit, he knows it,
but then a flat on the sink estate with a habit
isn't a great deal different
and you can't feed yourself on a giro.
it's a choice between cider, food and glue.
food doesn't numb despair like the others do,
begging doesn't hurt
once you've swallowed your pride
and you do what you have to do to get by.

paul stumbled into annie a year or so ago.
he was smashed on special,
remembers snow,
the fumes of the beer all thick in his head,
then annie knocked him dead.
a vision blown in from ireland
in tracksuit-top and worn-out jeans,
soaking wet, shivering in the breeze.
asked him for a cigarette

50

she was too frozen stiff to hold,
they shared his beer against the cold.
and then his bed. he said
"have you ever tried glue?"
to get by you do what you have to do.

they've been an item ever since.
there's been ups and downs
like you'd expect, but if you bump into one,
chances are the other one's around,
trying to make a few quid
by begging for coppers,
pissed on something cheap,
buoyed up with poppers.
the social workers blame paul.
they say he did wrong,
annie didn't know what drugs were
till he came along.
but their explanations are way too easy.
so paul saw her first,
so what? he just recognised the thirst
like anyone would have.
he saw the need for love and home
running through her,
a look he knew from his pitted bathroom
mirror,
and he knew he'd be safe with annie.
and that was enough.
and he hasn't brutalised her,
hasn't pimped her out
like some would have.
he knows she cares about
him, and he cares about her,
and that's as near as dammit to love.
and yeah, so, they do glue.

they're just doing what they have to do
to get through.
they prop each other up so that neither of
them falls.
it may not seem like much, but believe me
they give each other more
than anyone else has ever done.
they share their laughter, the cider,
and the glue,
look out for each other the best they know
how to.

paul says he'd die for annie
and he probably will.
last week, round at her place,
someone tried to kill
him with a blade.
he's got a punctured lung,
and could easily be dead,
says some bloke got fresh with ann,
and had a knife,
and tempers flare to nightmare
when everyone's off their head.
he's scared now.
he knows enough to see
that they're painted in a corner
and it doesn't matter how well they fight it
no-one really gives a shit
about them. there's no way out.
this isn't a movie
and the cavalry won't come galloping
over the horizon to save them.
that's how it is.

and they get out of it, get high,
do what they have to do to get by.

fuck it, says paul, choking back fear,
smiling at annie,
just fuck it.

calling a spade
a spade.

you saying
       you can have them as friends
       you just don't get involved.

me thinking
       i don't believe this.

you saying
       and the kids:
       neither one thing
       nor the other.

me saying
       no irish no blacks no dogs
       that's what they said.
       no irish. no blacks. no dogs.
       we're all immigrants,
       all in this together.

you saying
       no. we're white.

the words banging in my head
and me not saying anything
not believing this.

and then i say
       this   is   racism.

and you saying

54

no. it's not.
it's not racism.

and me thinking
so what shall we call it then?

gardening?

addiction.

you used to be my friend. i looked up to you,
and i wasn't the only one. a lot of people did.
you were the funniest, wittiest, most savage
person i think i'd ever met, holding court in
the pub, recounting the latest impossible tales
from the last tour in europe, making them all
come alive and true. weaving reality and
fiction together, but seamlessly, beautifully,
as all good storytellers do. the way you told
it, even a visit to the dss was an adventure.
man you were so full of life... i'd walk out at
the end of the night and my head would be
spinning with the intensity of it....

now i can't believe how you've changed.
can't believe you've stopped dreaming. can't
believe how everything you say is bullshit.
and i can't explain what i think i'm doing
here, round at yours with half a dozen cans
of your favourite lager, except maybe looking
for the friend i used to know.

and i say "look! stella! ice-cold!" and we
crack open a can each and sit on the floor of
your lounge, which is shabbier than i
remember, and i drink, and you don't, you
just keep rolling cigarettes, and i talk, and
nothing i say reaches you, and nothing you
say rings true. and after an hour or so of this,
i want to bang you up against a wall, scream
in your face, shake you till your teeth rattle,
get through to you for a moment so you'll do

more than just nod at whatever i say and roll
another cigarette and think about the next hit
while you wait for me to go.

but you want to pretend that life's just as it
always was, so i sit there and pretend so too,
until i've drunk all of the cans i brought
round for us to share, apart from the one
sitting on the floor beside you, the one you
opened as soon as i got here and haven't
touched since then, and never will, your
current taste in drugs being what it is, and i
look at it going to waste, and sod it, i ask for
it, and you give me a look like hey i was
about to start on that myself, and wait for me
to say ok fine, but i don't, and you hand it
over like you're doing me a favour, muttering
something about going to the shops in a
while to buy some more.

which is too much, and which somehow
combines with the fury and frustration and
the beer and the sadness, and i find myself
doing the one thing i undoubtedly shouldn't,
telling you that i've cried over you nights,
cried to watch you throwing it all away, cried
because you were my friend once, a long
long time ago.

and you look me straight in the eye for the
first time in what must be months, and say
how we all have our addictions, as if it
doesn't matter, as if that makes it all ok, and i
think yeah, so maybe we have. god knows i
can self-destruct as spectacularly as the next

man, and maybe i kid myself when i say it's
all under control, just like you do, but man, i
say, at least we should go down fighting, at
least we should try. but not this, not this.

and you shrug your shoulders and roll
another cigarette, as if i'm not talking about
your life or mine, or anything important.

and i go down the pub and drink till i've no
more money, and try picking fights with
strangers, insulting all my friends

all the time thinking it shouldn't be like this.

it shouldn't be like this....

police and thieves.

our police are wearing body armour. you
probably knew that anyway, but in case you
didn't, i'll say it again: west yorkshire's
finest are wearing body armour as a matter of
routine. watching them make an arrest now is
unreal, film-like. it's nypd on the streets of
our cities.

i mentioned this to a friend and he shrugged
and said we'll get used to it. and i suppose
we will. but that's not the point. read the
newspaper reports about the drugs war in
toxteth, look at the photos of police with
automatic weapons cruising the streets. think
about that. imagine how shocked by it you
would have been ten, even five years ago.
and now? barely a ripple of concern. muted
mutterings about a police state from the
predictable quarters, but for the most part,
nothing.

now this could be a sign of unexpected
maturity on the part of the great british
public, accepting and understanding the need
for the police to protect themselves from an
increasing danger of assault, and it would be
reassuring to believe that's what it is. but
maybe, just maybe it's the legacy of thatcher,
who declared there is no such thing as
society, that we don't really care overmuch
what happens in toxteth or elsewhere, so
long as it doesn't happen to us. or we do

care, but we've watched our fights come to nothing: against pit closures, nhs cutbacks, the criminal justice act, increasing privatisation. all of them failed. and we're exhausted. we feel powerless. and police and thieves become just so much tabloid gossip and vicarious horror.

i mean it's overwhelming, isn't it? you're trying to make ends meet in an economy that seems constantly on the edge of recession or worse, and here i am asking you to take on board the implications of police wearing body armour. too much. just thinking about thinking about it is enough to make you despair.

so it seems easier not to think about what's happening to our world, and that's what we do. we channel huge amounts of energy into not thinking about it, devote leisure time to not thinking about it, hell, not thinking about it can become a full-time occupation if you let it. there's a whole not-thinking-about-it industry developing in this country; it's probably one of the few growth industries we have....

which brings me back to the police, and their body armour. think about it. go on, let yourself. and maybe you'll find yourself getting angry, maybe you'll wonder who wins here? who loses? maybe you'll wonder what the bigger picture is, why these things are happening. and maybe that will be a start,

and you'll claim back some sort of small
control over your life.
and maybe not, of course, maybe not. there's
no guarantees here. except that anything,
anything has to be better than a world of
spoon-fed bigmacpepsimtv culture for those
lucky enough to belong, and armoured police
with machine guns for those who aren't part
of the dream

doesn't it??

voodoo.

they say voodoo only works if the intended
victim **believes** in the power of magic to
work its intended effect.

as if the shaking of a few old bones and a
ritual chant can damn you forever.... i mean
please, it's just too mad.

but maybe whenever you say you're
unlovable, stupid, ugly; each time you tell
yourself that criminals are born that way;
whenever you hear the voices of your
childhood telling you you'll never amount to
anything, or you do something for yourself
and believe you're doing wrong; then just
look at you. standing in the coolest club,
wearing the latest clothes, and drinking that
unbelievably hip beer, the one that's all the
craze for the next six months till a new one
comes along, and for all your claims to
sophistication, what are you doing? you're
believing in voodoo. letting it mess up your
life. listening to those dead old bones rattling
in the darkness of the night.

and it's so hard to break free, so easy to
excuse. say the odds were stacked against
you, you were stitched up from day one. you
watch your dreams slip by, telling yourself
they're unreachable. i know, i know... in a
different world, man, a different time, oh you
could have been a contender - but you've got

so used to being powerless, and you give the
strength to voodoo you should be keeping for
yourself.

and imagine
if you kept that strength
how there would be no-one else to blame
once you had made your life your own,
and in the thrill of the stillness after the
rattling of the bones,

imagine the great things which might be
possible.

and now the hardsell....

if you have enjoyed this book
and would like information
about any future readings or performances
by steve,
please write to:

p.o. box hp103
leeds. ls6 1ue.

enclosing an s.a.e.

his previous book,
"shattered",
also published by ak press,
is available from the above address
or can be ordered through
most good bookshops.